# Clark

## by Murray Ogilvie

# Lang**Syne**

## PUBLISHING

WRITING *to* REMEMBER

LangSyne

**PUBLISHING**

WRITING *to* REMEMBER

Vineyard Business Centre,
Pathhead, Midlothian EH37 5XP
Tel: 01875 321 203 Fax: 01875 321 233
E-mail: info@lang-syne.co.uk
www.langsyneshop.co.uk

Design by Dorothy Meikle
Printed by Montgomery Litho, Glasgow
© Lang Syne Publishers Ltd 2011

ISBN 978-1-85217-290-9

# Clark

*Echoes of a far distant past*
*can still be found in most names*

*Chapter one:*

# Origins of Scottish surnames

by George Forbes

## It all began with the Normans.

For it was they who introduced surnames into common usage more than a thousand years ago, initially based on the title of their estates, local villages and chateaux in France to distinguish and identify these landholdings, usually acquired at the point of a bloodstained sword.

Such grand descriptions also helped enhance the prestige of these arrogant warlords and generally glorify their lofty positions high above the humble serfs slaving away below in the pecking order who only had single names, often with Biblical connotations as in Pierre and Jacques.

The only descriptive distinctions among this peasantry concerned their occupations, like Pierre the swineherd or Jacques the ferryman.

The Normans themselves were originally Vikings (or Northmen) who raided, colonised and eventually settled down around the French coastline.

They had sailed up the Seine in their long-boats in 900AD under their ferocious leader Rollo and ruled the roost in north east France before sailing over to conquer England, bringing their relatively new tradition of having surnames with them.

It took another hundred years for the Normans to percolate northwards and surnames did not begin to appear in Scotland until the thirteenth century.

These adventurous knights brought an aura of chivalry with them and it was said no damsel of any distinction would marry a man unless he had at least two names.

The family names included that of Scotland's great hero Robert De Brus and his compatriots were warriors from families like the De Morevils, De Umphravils, De Berkelais, De Quincis, De Viponts and De Vaux.

As the knights settled the boundaries of

their vast estates, they took territorial names, as in Hamilton, Moray, Crawford, Cunningham, Dunbar, Ross, Wemyss, Dundas, Galloway, Renfrew, Greenhill, Hazelwood, Sandylands and Church-hill.

Other names, though not with any obvious geographical or topographical features, nevertheless derived from ancient parishes like Douglas, Forbes, Dalyell and Guthrie.

Other surnames were coined in connection with occupations, castles or legendary deeds. Stuart originated in the word steward, a prestigious post which was an integral part of any large medieval household. The same applied to Cooks, Chamberlains, Constables and Porters.

Borders towns and forts - needed in areas like the Debateable Lands which were constantly fought over by feuding local families - had their own distinctive names; and it was often from them that the resident groups took their communal titles, as in the Grahams of Annandale, the Elliots and Armstrongs of the East Marches, the Scotts and Kerrs of Teviotdale and Eskdale.

Even physical attributes crept into surnames, as in Small, Little and More (the latter being 'beg' in Gaelic), Long or Lang, Stark, Stout, Strong or Strang and even Jolly.

Mieklejohns would have had the strength of several men, while Littlejohn was named after the legendary sidekick of Robin Hood.

Colours got into the act with Black, White, Grey, Brown and Green (Red developed into Reid, Ruddy or Ruddiman). Blue was rare and nobody ever wanted to be associated with yellow.

Pompous worthies took the name Wiseman, Goodman and Goodall.

Words intimating the sons of leading figures were soon affiliated into the language as in Johnson, Adamson, Richardson and Thomson, while the Norman equivalent of Fitz (from the French-Latin 'filius' meaning 'son') cropped up in Fitzmaurice and Fitzgerald.

The prefix 'Mac' was 'son of' in Gaelic and clans often originated with occupations - as in MacNab being sons of the Abbot, MacPherson and MacVicar being sons of the minister and MacIntosh being sons of the chief.

The church's influence could be found in the names Kirk, Clerk, Clarke, Bishop, Friar and Monk. Proctor came from a church official, Singer and Sangster from choristers, Gilchrist and Gillies from Christ's servant, Mitchell, Gilmory and Gilmour from servants of St Michael and Mary, Malcolm from a servant of Columba and Gillespie from a bishop's servant.

The rudimentary medical profession was represented by Barber (a trade which also once included dentistry and surgery) as well as Leech or Leitch.

Businessmen produced Merchants, Mercers, Monypennies, Chapmans, Sellers and Scales, while down at the old village watermill the names that cropped up included Miller, Walker and Fuller.

Other self explanatory trades included Coopers, Brands, Barkers, Tanners, Skinners, Brewsters and Brewers, Tailors, Saddlers, Wrights, Cartwrights, Smiths, Harpers, Joiners, Sawyers, Masons and Plumbers.

Even the scenery was utilised as in Craig, Moor, Hill, Glen, Wood and Forrest.

Rank, whether high or low, took its place with Laird, Barron, Knight, Tennant, Farmer, Husband, Granger, Grieve, Shepherd, Shearer and Fletcher.

The hunt and the chase supplied Hunter, Falconer, Fowler, Fox, Forrester, Archer and Spearman.

The renowned medieval historian Froissart, who eulogised about the romantic deeds of chivalry (and who condemned Scotland as being a poverty stricken wasteland), once sniffily dismissed the peasantry of his native France as the jacquerie (or the jacques-without-names) but it was these same humble folk who ended up over-throwing the arrogant aristocracy.

In the olden days, only the blueblooded knights of antiquity were entitled to full, proper names, both Christian and surnames, but with the passing of time and a more egalitarian, less feudal atmosphere, more respectful and worthy titles spread throughout the populace as a whole.

Echoes of a far distant past can still be found in most names and they can be borne with pride in commemoration of past generations who fought and toiled in some capacity or other to make our nation what it now is, for good or ill.

*Chapter two:*

# Origins of the name

**The name Clark originates from the Latin clericus which described a member of a holy order, or scholar or writer. In medieval times most writing was carried out by the clergy which meant churchmen were respected as scholars.**

Through the centuries it evolved into de Clerk, Clerk, Clark and Clarke among others. Prior to the fifteenth century it was common to describe a man by his first name and or his occupation. The best example of this practice can be found in the signatories to the Ragman Roll which included the following: Adam Clerk of Edinburgh, William Clerk of Berwickshire, William le fiz Alain Clerk of Berwickshire, Walter Clerk of Roxburgh, Pieres Clerk of Edinburgh and William Clerk of Lanark. The Ragman Roll was a record of the acts of fealty and homage which King Edward I of England forced Scotland's nobility and gentry to sign in 1296. Edward was known as The Hammer of the Scots because of his attempts to impose his rule on the land north of the border. Initially, Edward had planned to annex Scotland through marriage. His intention was for his son and heir Edward to marry Margaret the Maid of Norway. She was the daughter of King Eirik II of Norway and Margaret, daughter of King Alexander III of Scotland. The princess was born in 1283 and was sometimes known as Margaret of Scotland and was considered to have been Queen of Scots from 1286 until she died in 1290 with no successor. There were fears that without a clear-cut heir to the Scottish throne a power vacuum would develop and the country would descend into tribal war. In order to prevent this Edward was invited by the nobility and other power brokers of the time to rule on who would be the next king. In return he insisted on the signatures to the Ragman Roll.

While there were plenty of Clerks in the southeast and east of the country at that time, there were also Clarks in the north. Although there was no Highland clan of that name, it is frequently found among the Clan Chattan confederacy. This was a grouping of Highland clans who lived near each other. Their land lay mainly in east Inverness-shire and stretched from Inverness to Laggan in the south, and from Glenloy in the west to Glenshee and Invercauld in the east. It embraced the upper stretches of four of Scotland's main rivers — the Nairn, Findhorn, Spey and Dee. The confederacy operated in a mutually beneficial manner and came into existence in the fourteenth century—ironically as a result of King Edward's actions. Prior to that Clan Chattan disappeared in 1291 when the last of the line, Eva, married Angus, the sixth Chief of Clan MacKintosh. He, and other MacKintosh chiefs who followed him, then became Captain of Clan Chattan. After the signing of the Ragman Roll King Edward chose John Balliol as the next king of Scotland. However, Edward still had his eye on controlling Scotland and began to undermine King John. Scotland's nobility retaliated by signing a treaty of mutual assistance with France, which became

known as the Auld Alliance. This infuriated
Edward who invaded Scotland. The English army
was joined by disaffected Scots led by Robert the
Bruce, who felt he had a stronger claim on the
Scottish throne than Balliol. Clan Chattan sup-
ported Robert The Bruce because MacKintosh's
enemy, John Comyn was a Balliol ally. After the
war, which Balliol's forces lost, MacKintosh was
rewarded with Comyn lands in Badenoch. For the
next 400 years Clan Chattan grew and prospered
as a confederacy. The confederation consisted
of the MacPhersons, MacPhails, MacBeans,
Cattanachs, MacKintoshes and their cadet
branches the Shaws, MacCombies, Ritchies,
MacThomases and the Farquharsons. Other asso-
ciate families without blood ties were the
Davidsons, MacAndrews. MacGillivrays, along
with branches of the MacLeans, MacIntyres and
MacQueens. The Clarks appear to have been a
sept (under the protection) of the MacPhersons,
whose origins were also from the church. Mac-a-
Phearsain is the Gaelic for son of the parson. It
was also at around this time that the name Clerk

ceased to refer solely to an occupation and became used a surname in its own right. Apart from the various anglicized spellings there was also a Gaelic version, Chleirich, and Mac a'Chleirich (son of the clerk) which evolved into McCleary, or more commonly, Clarkson.

*Chapter three:*

# Royal scandal

**Sir James Clark was born in 1788, in Cullen, Banffshire and rose to become Queen Victoria's physician. However, his close involvement in one of Victorian Britain's most infamous scandals almost put paid to his brilliant career.**

The case involved Lady Flora Hastings, who was the daughter of the Earl of Loudoun. She was brought up at Loudoun Castle, near Galston, Ayrshire and became a Lady-in-Waiting to the Duchess of Kent, who was the mother of Queen Victoria. One day Queen Victoria saw Lady Flora climbing into a carriage with Sir John Conroy, an Irish adventurer who was widely rumoured to have been the Duchess of Kent's lover and Victoria's natural father. The Queen noticed that a few months later Lady Flora appeared pregnant and confronted her. In those days a girl's purity was a major issue and losing one's virginity prior to marriage was unacceptable for anyone with close Royal connections. Despite Lady Flora's protestations the Queen was unmoved and insisted that she undergo a rigorous medical examination. Sir James Clark was called in. At the time it was thought Clark mistakenly pronounced her pregnant and did so because he had little experience of treating women. The consequences were disastrous for all concerned. The unfortunate Lady Flora was suffering from a cancerous growth in her liver, which had led to the swelling in her stomach. The treatment she had received at the hands of the Queen seriously damaged the monarch's popularity. There was a great public outcry against the Queen and eggs were openly thrown at the royal carriage. Lady Flora died in her sleep due to her illness, without receiving an apology from the Queen. Lady Flora's sister Sophie, whilst waiting by her death bed, refused to sleep in a bed belonging to the Queen. In addition, the family attached postage stamps, bearing the Queen's head, upside down. Sir James Clark became seriously tainted by the affair. He became unpopular and lost many of his patients. But it wasn't his fault. He had made an accurate diagnosis which was not publicised by the Queen. It was years before the emergence of the truth — that if his advice had been accepted, Lady Flora's honour would have survived. Eventually it became public knowledge that he had been wrongly blamed. Clark had progressed to the dizzy heights of Royal physician, before the Lady Flora affair, thanks to a combination indefatigability and genius. After graduating from Aberdeen University he originally hoped for a law career, but was drawn to medicine, which he studied at Edinburgh University. In 1809, although not a medical school graduate, he became a member of the Royal College of Surgeons of Edinburgh and joined the navy. His first two assignments may have deterred lesser mortals. His first appointment, in 1810, was as assistant surgeon aboard *HMS Thistle*. When the ship was wrecked off the coast of New Jersey Clark returned to England, was promoted to surgeon, and joined the *HMS Collobree*, which was also wrecked. Clark was not put off and served on two more vessels until

the end of the Napoleonic Wars in 1815. He then
continued his studies at Edinburgh University,
graduating MD in 1817. The following year he
took a close professional interest in phthisis,
which was the name given to tuberculosis (or pul-
monary consumption) at that time. In 1819 he settled in Rome, the resort frequented by many of the
higher echelons of English society, where he built
up a practice and a steadily increasing reputation
over the next seven years. During the summers he
visited various European centers and acquainted
himself further with the English aristocracy. On a
visit to Carlsbad he met Prince Leopold, later to
become King of the Belgians, who appointed
Clark his personal physician. Clark returned to
London in 1826, and three years later published
*The Influence of Climate in the Prevention and
Cure of Chronic Diseases, more particularly of
the Chest and Digestive Organs*, which was
described as his most influential work. In it he
gave the most accurate explanation yet of the
powers of climate and of mineral waters in the
treatment of disease. The book established his

reputation throughout the capital, where he used mineral waters to treat patients. He became popular with his patients because he went to the trouble of masking the nauseous taste of the drugs. In 1834 he was appointed physician to the Duchess of Kent. Among his duties was caring for the young Princess Victoria. When she became the Queen in 1837 he was appointed her physician in ordinary, and was created baronet. When she married in 1840 Sir James was also appointed physician to the Prince Consort, Prince Albert. He retired in 1860 and died ten years later.

*Chapter four:*

# Famous Clarks

**Given their geographical history, it's not surprising that another famous member of the Clark clan hails from the northeast of Scotland. Robert Clark was born in September 1882 in Aberdeen and is remembered for his role in the ill-fated Imperial Trans-Antarctic Expedition of 1914 which was led by Ernest Shackleton.**

After Aberdeen Grammar School Clark graduated from Aberdeen University with an MA and followed up with a B.Sc. In 1911 he became Zoologist to the Scottish Oceanographical Laboratory, Edinburgh, and two years later was appointed naturalist to the Plymouth Marine Biological Association. A year later, on August 9, 1914 the *Endurance* left Plymouth, carrying Shackleton and his crew. Their mission was to become the first to cross Antarctica from the Atlantic to the Pacific via the South Pole. Clark was chosen from around 5000 applicants. He was a hard worker with a dour manner. Although respected by his shipmates, he was also the victim of their practical jokes. On one occasion the crew boiled some spaghetti and placed it in one of his collecting jars. Clark, thinking he'd discovered a mysterious new species got very excited until the truth dawned.

But that was a minor setback comnpared to what would come next. Clark was meticulous in cataloguing the specimens caught up in the ship's nets. But the *Endurance* became trapped in ice and had to be abandoned. Clark was forced to leave all his work behind. Had he been able to salvage the collection it would have proved invaluable back home. The crew abandoned ship and set out on three lifeboats for Elephant Island. Clark was among those who waited there to be rescued by Shackleton and five others who had continued on to South Georgia for help. It took four months for Shackleton to return. Once he got safely back home Clark returned to Scotland where he married Christine Ferguson. He served as a Lieutenant on minesweepers in the Royal Naval Volunteer

Reserve during World War I and then returned to Plymouth in 1919. In his younger days he had been selected to play cricket for Scotland. He was recalled to the side in 1924. The following year he became a Doctor of Science and took over as director of the Fisheries Research Laboratory in Torry, Aberdeen. In 1934, he was appointed Superintendent of Scientific Investigations under the Fishery Board for Scotland. He retired in 1948 and died two years later at home in Murtle, Aberdeenshire. He had no children.

One of the Clarks became famous the world over, but he was not known by his original name. Dugald Clark was born in Glasgow in 1854. He had hoped to become a chemical engineer and studied at the Andersonian College, which is now part of Strathclyde University. However after leaving full-time education he chose a career in mechanical engineering. In 1877 he began working on a new invention which was destined to leave a lasting impression. Four years later he patented the world's first two-stroke engine, which was used for large gas and small petrol engines. By 1886 Clark was established in Birmingham, conducting gas-engine research and a partner in a successful consultancy. One of his clients was Frederick Lanchester, for whom Clark patented an engine starter in 1890. Thanks to him Clark became involved in the UK's fledgling automobile industry. He become the second president of the Institute of Automobile Engineers and his expertise was used in early automobile trials. As an authority on internal combustion engines, he led engineering research during the First World War and was appointed director of engineering research for the British Admiralty in 1916. He worked for the Trench Warfare Committee, which relied on his knowledge of designing ammunition-making machinery. At the Admiralty Research Department his knowledge of diesel engines was particularly appropriate in a new age of submarine warfare. His engine design was adopted by General Motors in the USA and used to form the Detroit Diesel Company. Clark received many honours for his work. He became a Fellow of the Royal Society, which is a learned society for sci-

ence that was founded in 1660. They presented
him with the Albert Medal, awarded for distin-
guished merit in promoting Arts, Manufactures
and Commerce. In 1917 he was knighted for his
wartime contribution. Yet all those honours were
bestowed upon Dugald Clerk, which is the way his
name was spelled in London. The consultancy he
formed in Birmingham with George Marks
became known as Marks and Clerk. It is still in
existence today. It is described as one of the
world's leading patent and trade mark attorney
firms with 80 partners and 400 employees. He died
in 1932 and to this day in Scotland, and particularly at Glasgow University where his papers are
archived, his name is spelled Clark.

Robert Clark, the son of a Montrose solic-
itor who started work in a law printer's office in
Edinburgh at the age of 13, revolutionized printing in Scotland. At 21 he borrowed £200, and
moved into a workshop in George Street. In
November 1864, he designed and produced a cir-
cular which was sent out to those connected with
the legal profession in the city offering his services

as a law printer. The business prospered, thanks mainly to orders from the Court of Session. Robert Clark was ambitious and was forever looking for ways to expand. On a trip to London he made useful contacts with some of the country's biggest publishers and returned to Edinburgh with a number of orders to print books. Before long Robert Clark was printing some of the world's biggest names including Robert Louis Stevenson, Bernard Shaw, Hugh Walpole, Thomas Hardy, HG Wells and WB Yeats. Clark's innovative streak was not confined to the end product. In 1871, during a strike in the printing industry he decided that to safeguard the company from future such disruptions he would train women to do what until then had been essentially a man's job. He undertook the task himself and Fanny MacPherson became the first woman compositor in Britain. She worked for Clark for 60 years and passed on her skills to other women. Clark died a very wealthy man at the age of 69 in March 1894 and his company was doing business with the biggest publishers in Britain. In 1946 the company was gifted to the University of Edinburgh. Roughly 40 years later, after a management buy-out and a merger gone wrong, it was no longer in existence.

No history of the Clarks is complete without an entry for Grand Prix legend Jim Clark OBE. He was born James Clark Jr. on March 4 1936 into a farming family at Kilmany House Farm, Fife, the youngest child of five, and the only boy. In 1942 the family moved to Edington Mains Farm, near Duns, Berwickshire. He was 20 before he took part in his first race, but his rise to the top of the motor racing world was meteoric. By 1958 he was driving for the local Border Reivers team, racing Jaguar D-types and Porsches in national events, and winning 18 races. On Boxing Day that year he finished second in a race to Colin Chapman, who was so impressed he signed Clark to his Lotus racing team. In 1961, in just his second Formula One season, he was involved in one of motor racing's worst accidents. In the Italian Grand Prix at Monza, Wolfgang Graf Berghe von Trips in his Ferrari collided with

Jim Clark's Lotus. Trips' car became airborne and crashed into a side barrier, fatally throwing von Trips out of the car and killing 15 spectators. Two years later Clark was World Champion. He'd won seven of the ten Grand Prix races and provided Lotus with its first Constructors Championship. He was World Champion again in 1965 and in the same year won the Indianapolis 500, becoming the only driver to achieve that double honour. He died on April 7, 1968. He should have been racing at Brands Hatch but instead drove in a minor Formula 2 race for Lotus at the Hockenheimring in Germany, due to contractual obligations. On the fifth lap his Lotus 48 veered off the track and crashed into the trees, killing him instantly. The cause of the crash was never definitively identified, but investigators reckon a faulty rear tyre was to blame. During his short career, he won 25 Grand Prix races and had achieved 33 pole positions. At that time it was more than any driver in history. He was buried in the village of Chirnside in Berwickshire.

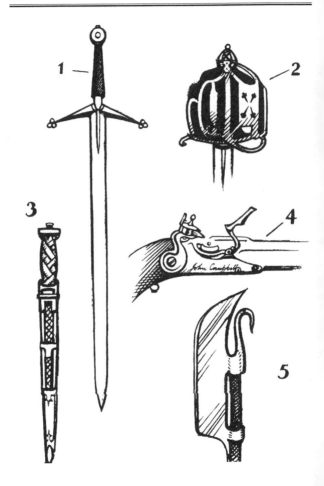

# Highland weapons

1)      The claymore or two-handed sword
        *(fifteenth or early sixteenth century)*

2)      Basket hilt of broadsword
        made in Stirling, 1716

3)      Highland dirk
        *(eighteenth century)*

4)      Steel pistol *(detail)* made in Doune

5)      Head of Lochaber Axe as carried
        in the '45 and earlier